My Grandfather's Love

*Keys to Happiness and Success
From Birth to Death and Beyond.
(For the Young and the Old)
Adventure, Pain, Victory*

The Life of William Thomas Williams
February 17, 1891 to May 23, 1983

●Teaches Godly Character, Moral Values and Principles

●This Book Is Recommended
for People of All Ages. It Is Easy Reading

By Craig Williams

© Copyright 1993 — Craig Williams

All rights reserved. This book is protected under the copyright laws of the United States of America. This book may not be copied or reprinted for commercial gain or profit. Short quotations or occasional page copying for personal or group study is permitted and encouraged. Permission will be granted upon request. Unless otherwise identified, Scripture quotations are from The King James Version of the Bible.

Take note that the name satan and related names are not capitalized. We choose not to glorify him, even to the point of violating grammatical rules.

**Produced by Companion Press
P.O. Box 310
Shippensburg, PA 17257-0310**

for:

ISBN 1-56043-534-8

For Worldwide Distribution
Printed in the U.S.A.

Contents

Chapter		Page
	Foreword	iv
One	**Growing Up With Adventure**	1
	Godly Training	
	The Big Bang	
	Grandpa's Sports Addiction	
	The Rough Walk to School	
	The Runaway Kids	
Two	**Adventures of Early Adulthood** .	21
	The Mail Box Gang	
	The Bum's Life	
	The Cowdip Extravaganza	
	The Wilderness Life	
Three	**Courting and Married Life**	39
	The Single Life	
	The Wife of His Youth	
	Getting Started	
	The Fruit of the Womb	
	The Loss of a Loved One	
Four	**Later Generation Activities**	71
Five	**Old But Still Active**	77
	The Decaying, Yet Renewed Man	
	Day to Day Life	
	A Church Goer	
Six	**The Final Round**	89
	The Final Week at Home	
	A Week of Pain	
	Death and Victory	
Seven	**Keys to a Successful Life**	101

Foreword

Have you ever wondered why some people are happy, victorious and successful in life while others seem as if they can hardly get things together? Usually this condition carries over from generation to generation. You question what you will do or what you have done in life. Is life worth living? Will I succeed in life? Hopefully, as you read this book you will gain insight on how to live a meaningful and successful life.

This is a story of a man who lived a long, meaningful and successful life, one filled with hard times and good times, sad times and glad times, prosperous times and lean times. The man had some meaningful experiences and some not so meaningful. Yet through it all he maintained peace, health, happiness and success, and he gave much to the world he lived in. What more could you ask for in life?

He learned that it is not how much you have, but what you do with what you have that is important. He learned that living and giving of oneself to things with eternal value proves to bring far more happiness than do things with no eternal value—things that decay and pass away with time. My prayer is that you will develop traits of eternal value, such as godly character and principles. As you read this book, remember that one has only one life to live and it will pass quickly. Only what's done for Christ in that life will last.

Proverbs 3:21 and 22 tells us to: "Have two goals: wisdom—that is, knowing and doing right—and common sense. Don't let them slip away, for they fill you with living energy, and bring you honor and respect." (Living Bible)

Special Thanks

To my heavenly Father who is full of love, mercy, and truth and to my wife Cathy and daughters Julie and Hannah.

Dedication

Dedicated in loving memory of my Mom, Peggy Lorraine Williams, who now lives in Heaven.

Chapter One

Growing Up With Adventure

Godly Training

My Grandpa's parents were God-fearing people, and their children and grandchildren were, too. We reap what we sow from generation to generation. Habits and characteristics, either good or bad, are picked up and handed down to our children. However, man is a free mortal agent, and he will choose whom he will serve and follow, whether it be God or man.

My dad once told me that there are only two churches in this world, God's and the devil's. A person is trained to live in either one or the other.

God's church is filled with righteous, loving, and submissive people. The devil's church is filled with evil, selfish, and rebellious people.

What we are taught while growing up, whether it be shameful sin or righteousness, will always be an influence on our lives. That's why we should be careful that we teach our children Godly principles and set examples that shows them right from wrong.

Grandpa's dad's name was George Comer Williams. His mom's maiden name was Alice Beacher Cole. It was their custom to take their children to church and make them sit with them. If the children would doze off during the service, their dad would thump them on the head. They would also take their children to Sunday School, revivals and singings. In these singings Christian people from all over the area would meet in various churches and perform for each other.

Back then the singings were held once or twice a month. Everyone would participate in them. Grandpa and Grandma would encourage their children to sing in these events as well as to get involved in other church activities. They would teach them Bible principles that would apply at home and abroad. Oh, yes, they definitely taught their children to serve God.

Grandpa's dad was a farmer. He taught his children to work hard and to be kind to others. He always

Growing Up With Adventure

took people in and fed them. He would put them up for the night and give them various jobs around the farm to help them out.

Of course, he also had plenty of jobs for his sons to do. He would keep them working in the garden—weeding, planting seed or harvesting. Often they would clear new ground and prepare it to be plowed and planted. Now farmers didn't just jump on their John Deere tractors in those days. They would hook up their plow and mule and head for the fields, and would work from sunup to sundown cutting down trees, pulling up stumps and burning brush. Firewood and posts were made from the trees that were cut down. Making posts was a vigorous job. First, the post was cut a certain length. Then a point was cut on one end so that it could be driven into the ground easily. Each post had to be treated with creosote so that it wouldn't rot. Fence lines were marked out, and posts were driven into the ground. Finally, barbed wire was stretched across the posts. This job went on and on, for they were continuously mending and repairing the fences.

Of course there were always chores to do; feeding and milking the cows, slopping the pigs, cleaning the barn—and the list goes on. This work was nothing unusual for the average farm boy in those days. It was expected of him and it was just part of his everyday duties.

The women did the cooking and the cleaning. They would cook on a wood stove and wash clothes in a tub with a scrub board. In later years gas stoves and washing machines became available. The women would raise chickens. They would trade eggs, vegetables, furs and whatever else they could with the peddlers who came around about once a week. They traded for salt, pots, cloth and many of their household and farm needs.

One thing for sure, with them staying so busy around the farm, they didn't have much time to get into trouble. This was the type of atmosphere in which they grew up. Working hard around the farm, and going to school and to church was their entire life. They participated in many activities at school and at church, and learned about God in the process. Not only did their parents teach them to live a holy life, but they also lived one before them.

Grandpa had four brothers, Grant, Carl, Walter and Sam, and one sister, Lizzie. Sam died of pneumonia when he was just three years old. Yes, he had quite some experiences with his brothers and sister.

Born on February 17, 1891, in the hills of Tennessee, Grandpa was given the name William Thomas Williams. In 1901, when he was at the ripe and mischievous age of ten, his family packed up to move to Florida. However, they were persuaded to move on to Louisiana when they heard that that state had plenty of land to homestead, and that the soil was great for farming there.

In Louisiana, his family first lived in Gonzales, where McDonalds and Burger King now stand. Back in those days it was just a field on the side of a bayou. The young people would do all sorts of things in that bayou. They would catch fish, hunt and trap mink, beaver, otter, coon, deer, rabbit, and squirrel. There was more to do than just hunt and fish in that bayou. For instance, in the summer time, after a day of work in the hot fields, they would run to the bayou to take a swim and cool off. Swimming races and mud fights were common.

Grandpa's family raised cotton in Gonzales for a few years before moving in 1904 to Weber City, an area outside of Gonzales. In 1905 they moved again to Cedars Point, and from there to an area called Gold Place. Grandpa lived in that area for the rest of his life.

As I did, you might wonder how Gold Place got its name. Actually, there wasn't any gold there. Many years ago settlers moved from French Settlement, a town about thirty miles southeast of Baton Rouge, Louisiana, to what is called Loura Ridge, ten miles west of French Settlement. There they raised cotton. In their spare time they built race tracks where horse races, wheelbarrel races and various other types of races were held.

Some of the settlers moved a few miles further west. They raised cotton there also and found that they could get two bales of cotton per acre compared to one bale per acre at Laurel Ridge. Because of this high cotton yield, they called the area Gold Place.

In his childhood, Grandpa worked on the farm; and went to school and to church. His mother spent hours reading the Bible to him, teaching him Godly principles and helping him with his school work. Yes, it takes time to rear children, especially if you're going to rear them correctly.

Grandpa went to school in Gonzales, Weber City and St. Amant. There the teachers taught him the basic skills of reading, writing, and arithmetic. He was also encouraged to learn and memorize the Bible, to pray, and to love and respect his playmates and authorities. You might say it is a far cry from what it is like in most schools today.

He finished school in the ninth grade. In those days, that was all the schooling that was needed to graduate. You then either worked on the farm or found a job until you were married, went to college, or joined the service.

Grandpa said the teachers were good teachers back then. For instance, one time there was a bully at school who had already beaten up his brother Grant. One day as they were outside playing jump-rope—with a rope that was actually made from vines out of the trees in the area—the bully decided to pick on Grandpa. He had a long vine and Grandpa had a short one. For some reason the bully came after Grandpa, swinging his vine. When Grandpa saw this, he ducked under the bully's vine and got up close so that the bully couldn't hit him hard, because his vine was too long. Grandpa just lit into him with his short vine and gave him a good licking. The bully learned an important lesson—it doesn't pay to pick on other people.

Because of this incident, Grandpa skipped school for the next few days. He was afraid of what the teacher might do to him. In the morning he would walk part of the way to school, find a shade tree to sit under, play around until his brothers came back that evening, and then walk home with them. The teacher discovered where he was and sent two of the older students to get him. He didn't know what to expect when he arrived at school. Would it be a whipping or a tongue lashing in front of the other students? To his surprise, it was neither. The teacher sat him in her lap and talked the situation over with him. She explained the right way and the wrong way to handle the situation. Grandpa said he really learned to like and respect her after that, for she took the time to understand his fears and problems. So many times parents get upset and whip a child without taking the time to look over the situation, and without explaining the rights and wrongs to their child.

Growing Up With Adventure

This is one of the things that has caused a lot of hatred, distrust, misunderstanding and communication problems in families. Parents have accepted their responsibility to feed and clothe their children, while failing to teach them godly moral principles based on love and understanding. Don't just punish your child; when he makes a mistake, let him know that what he did was wrong, how it can harm him, and what he can do to avoid letting it happen again. By all means, set an example for your children by the way you live. Install eternal values in your children by word and deed.

Grandpa learned some important lessons from his teachers. For instance, he learned that it doesn't pay to be mischievous in class. First of all, if you are mischievous, you don't learn anything, and secondly, as Grandpa found out, you get into trouble. One day at school Morris Bourgeois was sitting in front of Grandpa. Morris dropped his pen and as Grandpa picked it up, he got a wild idea. He looked at Morris, then at the pen, and stuck Morris in the bottom end with it. Needless to say, Morris let out a loud scream and liked to jumped clean out of his seat, as did the rest of the students.

The teacher was standing right there at the scene of the crime and didn't quite agree with the move Grandpa made. She spanked Grandpa's hand, made him write lines, and stay after school. Grandpa learned that he had better not do just anything that pops into his mind, because he could end up regretting it. It would solve a lot of our problems if we would learn to use some foresight in our decisions. Look ahead to determine what the final outcome of your decision will be. We must also be humble and open to correction so that we can learn from our mistakes.

As for transportation to and from school, you should be thankful for the cars and busses that you have to ride today. Grandpa told me that back then they had to walk to school and back, two to four miles. Sometimes they would ride horseback. He talked about an early type of school bus they used, a covered wagon pulled by horses. His brother came up with the idea one day when it was raining. By riding the wagon, they wouldn't get wet and they could all ride together and talk like children do on school busses today. They picked up their neighbors and took them to school also.

In looking at this example, I can see how people in those days tried to find ways to help others. But today you can hardly pay people to help someone. The word of God teaches us differently. It tells us not to be selfish, to help others, and to love them as we do ourselves.

As Grandpa grew older, Godly principles were taught to him as his parents believed and lived by Proverbs 22:6: "Train up a child in the way he should go: and when he is old, he will not depart from it." I pray that your child will grow up to be a person with Godly principles.

Grandpa definitely had some adventures as he grew up. He has shared some of them with me and now I would like to share them with you.

The Big Bang

Grandpa had quite an experience with gunpowder when he was a young lad of around seven years old. One day he and his brothers Grant and Walter were left at home alone. You know how children are—when the cat's away the mice will play. For some reason, children do things when they are alone that they wouldn't normally do if their parents were present. But the word of God tells us that our sins will find us out.

While looking for something to do, Grant spotted a musket his dad had told him not to fool with. As he looked at it he wondered what it would be like to shoot it. He found some gunpowder and eagerly began to load the musket. In the process, he spilled the gunpowder and made a big mess. In the meantime, Grandpa had found some matches. When he saw Grant trying to load the musket, he and Walter gathered around to observe and wait for the big bang.

However, Grandpa dropped a lighted match into the freshly-spilt gunpowder, and the big bang came a lot quicker and with a lot more force than they had expected. The gunpowder ignited with a very destructive force. Grandpa and his brothers were all badly burned and could have lost their lives, but God spared them. Grandpa's right hand and nose were burned and he had the scars to show for it. That experience helped them to see that their parents had a reason for telling them not to do certain things. Their parents learned that they shouldn't leave their children at home alone.

God spared Grandpa's life, just as he has spared my life many times and has probably spared yours many times, also. For what were we spared? Revelation 4:11 says for his pleasure we were created. We can give pleasure to our heavenly Father by the way we live. It pleases Him if we live a righteous life of love, giving praise and honor unto Him. One of the reasons He is pleased is because others see His love and righteousness in us and come to Him. This is God's desire, that all come to him and that none should perish. But it displeases God if we live in sin, because it separates us from God and leads others away from Him. However, it is our duty to present ourselves a living sacrifice, holy and acceptable unto God our creator through Jesus Christ, the one mediator between God and man. (See Romans 12:1 and I Timothy 2:5.)

Grandpa's Sports Addiction

Most young boys today get involved in some sort of sport, whether it be football, basketball, baseball,

Growing Up With Adventure

racing or something else. They always find some kind of competition to get into, either on a formal team or just in the back yard playing with friends and cousins.

Well, it was no different in Grandpa's day. One activity that he was pretty good at was running races. One day there was a big race in a nearby city in which he was to take part. His dad was very proud of how well he was doing in the races, and decided to buy him a fancy running suit as a reward for his accomplishments. As he put on the suit, I'm sure he must have thought, "Boy I have arrived. I'm the big man on campus". But you know that the word teaches us that pride comes before a fall.

The day of the race arrived and they headed out for Donaldsonville. When they arrived, Grandpa walked around in his new suit with pride and joy. The time came for the race to start, and the participants lined up. They took off swiftly as the gun sounded. Suddenly, after about thirty yards Grandpa's feet got caught in his new long, loose running pants, and he came tumbling down, flip flopping all over. Yes, his heart was broken, his pride hurt and he was filled with embarrassment and sorrow, for his chance to win the big race was gone. He learned an important lesson about what kind of apparel to wear when racing and about what kind of attitude to have.

There is a lesson in this story for all of us. We must remember to give God the glory in our race through life and to put aside any extra weight or item that would hinder us from running and winning the most important race of all—the race through life that leads to eternal life.

Grandpa played ball quite often on Sunday afternoons. That was about the only time they had to play, because the rest of the time they were either working, or going to school or church. His cousins would get together, and they really got into it.

During these games Grandpa usually played catcher. One day as they were playing fast pitch, with Grandpa catching as usual, his cousin threw one of the fastest pitches he had ever thrown. Grandpa had his hand in the wrong position and the ball hit his finger and broke it. He had trouble with that finger the rest of his life.

The Rough Walk to School

When Grandpa was young and still going to school, he had many different experiences. He remembers walking to school one day with his brother through a black neighborhood. The first few times they walked that way some of the neighborhood boys chased them and roughed them up a little. It was an experience they did not enjoy. One evening as they were diligently working in the fields they came up with an idea. (It's funny how we come up with ideas when we are working that don't even pertain to our job.) As they were tilling the fields they dug up a root that looked like a pistol, and a brilliant idea popped into their heads. The next morning they got up, saddled a horse, and rode through the area where they had been chased. Sure enough, their friends came to challenge them. So Grandpa pulled out his root and when the boys saw it they mistook it for a pistol and turned and ran the other way. Needless to say Grandpa and his brother had a good laugh.

You know, this reminds me so much of satan. He makes us think he has a big stick or gun. We get afraid, worried and troubled but its just fake, and satan gets the laughs. He even tries to make us think he possesses real life, but it is not real and it won't last. Even though we know that God is the creator of life, and that He alone gives life with real love, joy, peace and happiness that will last, we still believe satan's deception. I would like to say one thing in relationship to this story. Jesus tells us to love everybody and to be at peace with them regardless of their color or race. Instead of being prejudiced, we should have love for all men. If you can't love your fellow man you will never have peace inside. God wants to give you the love that never fails.

The Runaway Kids

One time, when Grandpa was around ten years old, he and Grant ran away. One day they were misbehaving at school, and the teacher made them stand on a bench in front of the room. The other students started laughing and making fun of them. This really embarrassed them. The teacher saw what was going on, but wouldn't do anything about it. On top of that, they knew their dad would give them a good whipping when they got home, so they figured, as many youth do, that it would be better to run from their problems instead of facing them and working them out. They decided that on the next recess they would set out for Texas, a hasty decision made without much foresight.

That's just what they did. The next recess they started walking down the road heading west. They were really enjoying themselves at first, playing chase and admiring the beautiful scenery. They talked of how they wouldn't have to listen to the teacher anymore. They wouldn't have to listen to their dad getting on them for not doing their chores or for getting in trouble at school. They wouldn't have to make their beds and do their homework. Oh, yes, they thought they had it made as they happily walked further and further away from home. After several hours they started getting tired and hungry. They wondered what they'd eat for supper. Then their minds wandered back home where the rest of the family was eating a fresh-cooked, hot meal. They thought of all the wonderful meals mom had cooked for them, and that made them even more hungry.

As darkness rolled in and they saw the birds finding their nests for the night, their minds were brought back to reality. They began to wonder where they would sleep that night. Would it be in the woods all alone with vicious animals, or would it be in someone's barn, fearing they would get caught? Their minds raced back to their nice cozy home where they could be protected from all harm. Yes, their adventuresome trip had brought some frightening facts to them. As they gazed off into the sunset they suddenly heard a voice saying: "Hey, what are you boys doing so far away from home?" Frightened, they turned around to see one of their neighbors returning home from a trip. As they stood there speechless, the man said, "I see you boys must have had some problems at home and decided to run away. You know, its a big responsibility to be on your own. You have to feed yourself, clothe yourself, get a place for shelter and protect yourself from wild animals. You think you boys can handle all that?" They looked at each other and said, "Probably so."

The neighbor said, "You have to *know*, because when you are out on your own there are so many things you have to be prepared for. That's why God gave you boys good parents. They teach, train and discipline you boys so that one day you can be on your own and will be able to handle the problems you face.

"I can't figure out what kind of problems would have made you run away from your lovely home. I'm sure if you would have prayed about it you could have come up with a solution to work out your problems. Did you even try to work them out?" Grandpa said, "No, I don't guess we did." "How would you like to go back home and work out your problems? You could ride with me since I'm heading that way," replied the neighbor. Grandpa said, "Yea, I guess we could work out the problems somehow."

The man took the boys home, arriving there late at night. Boy, their mom and dad were really worried, and were glad to see them. Their dad gave them a good talking to and sent them to bed. The next day he put them to shucking corn in the barn. The boys had learned some important things that day. They found that it isn't easy to be on your own. They also realized that their parents cared for them and understood them after all. Don't make hasty decisions without counting the cost. You will probably end up regretting it.

Chapter Two

Adventures of Early Adulthood

The Mail Box Gang

We should always try to find something constructive for our children to do. For if they are idle, they may find themselves in trouble. Grandpa must have taught my dad this, because we always had jobs to do around the house. I must admit it worked pretty well because we stayed out of trouble more than the average child. Even though we did manage to get into trouble a few times, we did learn a lot about responsibility, discipline, and work.

This leads to the story of the mail box gang. There was a group of boys who didn't have much to do. Once they got together and saddled up their horses and got some rope. As they rode along, they chatted about some of the good times they had had in the past. Darkness settled in as they rode on, seeking something to do. They rode past driveway after driveway, and dogs would chase them from time to time. Finally, one boy pulled out his rope and started swinging it as he went by a mail box. He pictured a calf running along the road, and he roped it. Then he pulled on the rope as if the mailbox were giving him a fight. His friends cheered him on until he finally pulled down the mail box. They cheered and got a big kick out of it. As they laughed, they pulled out their ropes, also, thinking it would be so much fun. They wondered if they would get in trouble for it. Should they, or shouldn't they do it? As they started daring one another, they finally gave into peer pressure and started pulling down mail boxes all over the area.

Along the way they pulled down Grandpa's mailbox. Guess what? Once wasn't enough. Grandpa put it back up and they pulled it down again a few nights later. This happened several times. So grandpa decided that he would make them work for their fun. He cemented his mailbox in the ground. The next time the gang got together they were in for a surprise. They were having a good old time until they got to Grandpa's. One boy roped the box and galloped off. When the rope reached its end, the horse, being frightened, reared up and the saddle flew off. The rider fell to the ground; and his friends raced off in fear, leaving him there alone. His heart was filled with fear that he would get caught as he rapidly gathered together his saddle and rope and fled the scene. Needless to say, that ended that adventure for them; but I'm sure they found another.

They were really blessed, for they could have been shot or seriously injured fooling around like that. Remember, it pays to keep your children busy with creative activities.

The Bum's Life

One day when Grandpa and a friend were around twenty years old they set out for a little town called Planneville, in Mississippi. They were looking for adventure and work, and they found both. After spending a few days in Planneville, they found a job in a factory. Grandpa and his friend, having been raised on a farm, weren't too familiar with the types of machines found in a factory. Yes, they knew all about mules, plows and other farm equipment; but the machinery of a factory was something new.

As Grandpa observed the men at work in the factory, he studied and learned how to operate the machinery. He was amazed. After watching for a few days, he figured there wasn't much to operating them, so he gave it a try. He found out that it wasn't as easy as he thought. He ended up catching one of the machines on fire and getting fired.

Adventures of Early Adulthood

After that experience they decided to head for home. They paid for the room where they had stayed, gathered what little belongings they had; and took a train to Hammond, Louisiana. From there they used what money they had left to take a train to New Orleans. It was late when they arrived, and they decided to find a boarding house and stay there for the night. They were just getting settled in when a bunch of guys came in, drinking and carrying on. The men insisted that Grandpa drink with them if he intended to stay there that night. He didn't want to drink; but in order to avoid trouble he pretended that he was. After a little while, they left him alone and mosied off to sleep.

The next morning Grandpa and his friend got up and set out by foot since they didn't have any money. After walking a few hours they started getting tired and hungry. Grandpa had some fishing line and a hook in his pocket. He found a good limb to use as a fishing pole. They looked for some bait, but couldn't find any, so for the fun of it Grandpa grabbed a blackberry and stuck it on the hook and threw it in. To his amazement it was no time before he had hooked a fish. It was a big one, too. He wrestled and struggled with it, trying not to break his pole. He finally pulled it in—a five pound catfish. Grandpa was very excited about that, and they started a fire and cooked the rascal. When it was ready, Grandpa and his friend thanked the

Adventures of Early Adulthood

Lord for blessing them with a catfish caught with a blackberry.

Now that they had a little food in their stomachs, they were ready to set out again. They had been following the railroad tracks, and were around the swamps just outside of New Orleans. There was still a long way to go, and as they walked along the tracks they hoped a train would come along that they could jump. When they came to a place where the trains stopped to get water, they hid in the woods and waited for one to come.

Finally, after waiting an hour or so they heard a train approaching. They stayed hidden as the train eased to a stop and started taking in water. With hearts pounding, they decided to make a run for it. They ran and climbed on top of one of the cars, but the conductor saw them and called them down. They tried to hide on top of the train, but it was too late. The man had seen them and kept hollering for them to come down. Finally, they climbed down and explained their situation to him. He asked if they had any money. They had a few nickels and pennies left so they gave them to him, and he let them ride in one of the empty cars. As they rode along getting closer and closer to home, they talked about the adventures of their trip, realizing that it was an unprofitable journey.

They had big plans of getting rich, yet here they were coming back with nothing riding in the cattle car of a train like a bum. Boy, were they glad when the train stopped in Gonzales. They jumped off the train and walked for about a mile to the Black Bayou bridge. At daybreak, they split up and went home where they would have a nice warm bed to sleep in and a good homecooked meal to eat, which was something they hadn't had in quite some time. They thought to themselves, "there's no place like home."

The Cowdip Extravaganza

One of the first stories that Grandpa shared with me was something that happened after he was married.

Grandpa lived most of his life around people who lived off the land, raising crops, cattle, and trading. One year the farmers' cattle became heavily infested with ticks. The government decided to help them out by constructing cowdips filled with treated water, and requiring the farmers to dip their cows once a week. (A cowdip is a cemented hole in the ground, sort of like a small swimming pool.) Well, do you know how much trouble it is to round up cattle that run loose on miles of land? It's not easy, but it had to be done every week.

The farmers tried it for a few weeks, but weren't seeing positive results. After all that hard work, they were kind of upset and discouraged. The government said that they had to keep doing it. The

Adventures of Early Adulthood

Adventures of Early Adulthood

farmers decided if this thing wasn't going to work, there was no sense in them bringing their cattle to these dips every week. Yes, they were stirred up; and decided to do something about it. They held an emergency meeting one night to discuss the matter. "Hey, we can't go on like this. We have to do something," they said, and decided that the best thing to do was to get rid of the cowdips. How could you get rid of cowdips? You couldn't tear them down piece by piece for they were made of concrete and it would take too long. But you could blow them up, and that's what they decided to do. The best and quickest way would to be destroy them with dynamite.

Several men were chosen to obtain the dynamite, and it was agreed to meet again a few nights later. Well, they got their dynamite and met again as planned. At the meeting place they were split up into pairs and assigned a cowdip to dynamite. Grandpa and his partner received their explosives, and before they knew it they were being driven down the road to their assignment.

As they approached their destination, they wondered what would happened to them if they were caught. Would they go to jail? Would they pay a fine? What if the dynamite didn't work? What if the dynamite blew up before they could get away from it? After all, the fuses were kind of short. They really started to sweat. At the cowdip the car stopped.

Adventures of Early Adulthood

Grandpa and his friend looked at each other and then at the driver, and crawled out of the car. The driver was supposed to wait for them there, but he got a little nervous thinking about the explosion and what could happen to him if he were caught, and he drove off and left the rest of his team there.

This did not discourage them, and they began to find their way through the dark woods to the cowdip. It was not an easy task to avoid the briars and to find their way through the dark. They managed, and finally reached the cowdip. To their surprise it was filled with logs. Someone had already tried to stop the operation of this cowdip. Grandpa and his partner reasoned that all someone had to do was clean out the logs and the dip would be in operation again, so they decided that they must blow it, anyhow.

They carefully planted the dynamite, lit the fuses, and ran for their lives. As Grandpa got up a full burst of speed he ran right into a briar patch. He began squirming desperately, trying to make his way through the briars, knowing that at any moment the dynamite would go off. About that time he heard a loud boom as the dynamite exploded. Logs went flying everywhere, falling all around Grandpa. By the grace of God, he wasn't hurt except for some scratches from the briars.

When everything settled down, they went back to the dip and examined it and decided that the job

Adventures of Early Adulthood

was successful. They began walking home, talking about the exciting night they had had, and of their plans for the next morning, for their job was not completely finished yet.

The next morning Grandpa woke up bright and early, and like the other farmers, he rounded up his cattle and herded them down to the nearest cowdip as if they knew nothing was wrong. When they arrived, to their amazement they discovered that the cowdips had been blown up. They discussed the matter, saying, "Who could have done such a thing?"

The government decided it would be too costly and too dangerous to rebuild the cowdips, so they left the farmers alone to tend to their own business. The farmers felt that their job was accomplished. In one way it was, but this hasty deed would come back to haunt them down the road, for they had lost the help and support of the government for the time being.

As Grandpa and his friends did, we often act in haste, wanting to do things immediately and in our own way. I tell you, if we could only learn to put our trust in our Heavenly Father who knows all things, if we could patiently and humbly seek Him for an answer to our problems, He would lead us to the best solutions for our problems and He would guide us to a life of joy, happiness and real freedom.

The Wilderness Life

I must say that life is an adventure and a wilderness experience, but what is important is what we make and learn out of our experiences. My Grandpa learned much from his. I want to share another of Grandpa's adventures with you.

This story recounts how Grandpa ventured out on his own for the first time. It occurred between the times when he finished school and when he was married. That is the time in life when many young men venture out alone for the first time. It is a very important time, a time of maturing and of accepting responsibility. It is a time when many learn a trade for life. This time can prove to be very valuable to a man as he approaches the next phase of his life.

One of the adventures that Grandpa faced during this time of his life was a winter spent in the swamps with his brother Grant and his cousin Red Singletary. They lived in a camp deep in the swamps, cut off from all civilization. As they paddled their pirogue to the camp that they had built the previous summer, they wondered what it was going to be like without their mother to cook their dinner, wash their clothes and do all the other things that mothers do. Well, they would soon find out.

They had built their camp walls out of logs, and used bark and palmetto and clay to make the roof.

They also used clay to construct a fire place. When they put fire to the clay, it became solid enough in which to burn wood and cook.

The men planned to live off of fish, squirrel, rabbit and whatever else they could catch or shoot. The hides of trapped mink and coon would provide them with a little money.

The first night found the adventurers getting settled in and preparing their fishing lines and traps for the next morning. Sleep didn't come easily that night, as animals and screech owls could be heard in the woods around them. The next morning they eagerly awoke, put on their warmest clothes, loaded their boats and set out for the morning. Trout lines and bushlines were set out and baited, and traps for coon, mink, beaver, and otter were carefully set out and marked. All morning was spent in these activities, and by the time they got back to their camp they were freezing and starving, and the campers wondered if they had made a mistake by coming into those swamps.

A fire was built, and they ate some of the grub they had brought with them. After a brief rest, the adventurers set out for the woods once more to kill some game—rabbit, squirrel, deer—so that they would have something to eat, for they knew that what they had brought with them wouldn't last long. They hunted for an hour or two and killed a

Adventures of Early Adulthood

few rabbits before returning to check their traps and fishing lines.

The catch was light that evening, for the lines had been out only for about a half-day and they hadn't been set with much care. The men anxiously went from trap to trap, line to line. They were a little discouraged, but they did manage to catch a few fish and an otter. They took their catch home and cleaned it. Enough firewood was gathered to last for the night, and they had rabbit for supper. When they finished dinner they were so tired from the day's activities that they went straight to bed. That night they like to froze to death, so they didn't sleep too well. The next morning they were up bright and early, ready to eat breakfast and check their traps. When it came time to cook breakfast, they found that all of their pots and pans were dirty, so they had to wash them. Finally they got a hardy breakfast down and started out for another day of adventure. This daily routine went on for the next two months.

In order to live in the swamps for a whole winter the men had to be brave, courageous, strong and use common sense. They also learned to meet responsibility and to do things that had to be done, for if they didn't, they did without.

Grandpa learned to dress properly and to keep an ample supply of firewood so that he wouldn't freeze to death. He also learned to hunt properly in order to keep a sufficient supply of food in the camp. He would walk quietly and patiently as he hunted his prey. He would set his traps at the right place and at the right time and would cleverly bait and hide them. He also learned to swiftly and properly skin his prey. He then learned to preserve the meat and skins of the animals he caught so that he could be sure to get good prices for them. The housekeeping chores such as cooking, cleaning, washing dishes, washing clothes, making beds, and sweeping floors all soon became part of his everyday duties.

He soon learned to keep plenty of covers on hand to keep him warm while sleeping. He also made sure that his clothes and boots were dry before wearing them. He burnt some of them by getting them too close to the fireplace. Even in his old age he still had the habit of doing that. You wouldn't imagine how many boots he burnt holes in while trying to keep his feet warm. He would come in from the garden, sit down and prop up his boots against the open space gas heater with the feet still in them. Before long you could smell rubber burning. I would wonder how he kept his feet in those hot boots. One day I went by his house and saw a pile of burnt stuff in the back yard. I couldn't figure out what it was. Grandpa said it was his boots. Those things had burnt slap up and I guarantee you that he didn't keep them on during the process. After that incident his sons Gyles and Hilton

Adventures of Early Adulthood

bought and hooked up an electric heater with guard rails on it so he wouldn't burn himself up.

Finally, the boys got tired of their stay in the swamps, so they prepared to go home. They gathered in all of their traps and fishing lines, dug up their salted meat and the furs that they had caught during the last few months, and loaded their pirogues. The vessels were loaded to the brim with furs, meat and supplies. The outdoorsmen gladly headed out of the swamps, for they had had enough of that kind of living to last them for a while.

Grandpa wound up making a hundred dollars from the sale of his furs, which went a long way back then. Of course, the lessons he learned about life through his experiences in the swamps were far more valuable than the money that he earned.

I heard an interesting saying one time that goes along with this story. It's very true and it goes like this.

"Give a man a fish and he will eat for one day. Teach a man to fish and he will eat for the rest of his life." (Author unknown.)

With this one hundred dollars Grandpa bought nine acres of land before going into the military.

Grandpa learned many things about life through his childhood experiences. However, if it wouldn't have been for his mom and dad giving him godly counsel, he might have molded a bad character and a bad attitude about life. Instead, he learned to trust in God and follow His guidance throughout his life. His upbringing also helped prepare him for the next phase of his life.

Chapter Three

Courting and Married Life

The Single Life

Grandpa was just like all the other young men, he desired to be married someday. God said it was not good for man to be alone so he made woman. For this cause shall a man leave his father and mother and shall cleave unto his wife and the two shall be one flesh. (See Genesis 2:24 and Matthew 19:5.) Being a single young person isn't always easy. Many times the adult world will not accept young singles as an adult and will not fellowship with them. Members of the younger generation tend to shun young singles also, because of the age

Courting and Married Life

difference. Young singles tend to fear to fellowship with the younger generation because of what the adult world may say and think. Yes, it's not always easy, but if you find yourself in that type of situation, God's grace and compassion will comfort you. You will feel lonely and unaccepted at times, but God loves you as you are. You will experience times of frustration and confusion, but hold on to Jesus and He will lift you up and give you understanding. He will provide companionship and friendship in His time.

If you are not called to be single you will always long and look for your life's partner. Remember the most important thing in your life is your personal, intimate relationship with God. The second is your personal, intimate relationship with your mate. If you can keep your personal relationship with God as the number one priority in your single life, you will find much happiness and fulfillment in life. Also, you will find the proper mate for you, for you will have God's direction and blessings upon your life.

Most of the young men of Grandpa's day were already married by the time he made up his mind to marry. At the age of twenty-six he finally found the wife of his youth. Some people say it's better if you wait a while before getting married. Some say the sooner the better. Well, Grandpa waited until he was older. I'm sure he had good reasons for waiting.

Courting and Married Life

He probably wanted to make sure he was mature enough and able to handle the responsibilities of marriage. He also wanted to make sure he had the right girl, because once he was married it was until death do them part.

At any rate, Grandpa led an active single life, a good thing for a single person to do. There's so much that can be accomplish during a person's single years. Instead of sitting around griping and moping and complaining because you haven't found the right mate, get out and do something with purpose to it. Find something with meaning to do, such as helping others, getting involved in church activities, or pursuing hobbies.

I would imagine that most people who sit around and gripe and mope because they can't find a mate are not only unhappy as a single person but also end up with an unhappy marriage, for they act in haste when they do find someone who is interested in them. Their motives for marriage are based on selfishness instead of true love. Don't be hasty to be married. Enjoy your single life and base your dating standards and relationships on God, because He created marriage and surely he can lead you to the right person, place and time for marriage.

Grandpa led an active single life. He stayed busy around the farm, tilling the land, mending fences, tending the livestock, hunting, fishing, going to

Courting and Married Life

church, dating, and even contrary to the way he was raised, going to bars occasionally.

One evening while visiting a bar he got into a fight, an event that happens quite often in such places. A Chinese guy said he didn't like Grandpa's looks and the way he talked, and he told him he wasn't Cajun enough and couldn't be from this area. Grandpa said, "No, I'm from Tennessee." For some reason this provoked the man. He grabbed a chair and said, "We will fight." Grandpa looked at him and said, "If we're going to fight, why don't you put down that chair and fight with your fists." The man put down the chair, but Grandpa picked it up and hit the man over the head with it. The blow knocked him out and that ended the fight.

As a single man Grandpa sometimes got involved in things that he shouldn't have been involved in. However, his parents still loved him and he continued to go to church. Well, this paid off, because God miraculously dealt with Grandpa. One night as he was riding his horse down around Hinderson Bayou, a light shown upon him. It scared him and his horse real good. The horse reared up and took off. When Grandpa got the horse back under control he tried to figure out where the light had come from, but couldn't. From that experience he felt the presence of God deep inside him. The Spirit of God began wooing him as he began searching his life. He felt there was a void in his life that needed to be filled.

Courting and Married Life

After several weeks had gone by, Grandpa forgot about the incident, but the Lord hadn't. One reason for this was because his mother was still praying for him. (Remember, prayer is a powerful force.) One night as Grandpa was riding home from church in the back of a wagon, the light appeared to him again. I'm sure at first it startled him, but again he realized deep inside that it was God getting his attention in a special, unique way.

As the wagon rolled on, the Spirit of God spoke to him and he began to recognize his sinful nature. He was sorry for sinning against God. As the Holy Spirit dealt with him, he acknowledged his sins before God, for he knew he had no excuses for them. He began renouncing them and putting them out of his life, knowing the shame they could bring him. He consecrated his life, and vowed to serve God from that day on if He would forgive him. A seed that had been planted in his heart and cultivated for many years sprouted and grew and brought new life to him by faith. He realized that God really did love him by sending his son Jesus to die for his sins. He knew that through Jesus he could have forgiveness of his sins and fellowship with God. From that point on he began a new life in Christ Jesus. No longer did he fear death, for he knew to die was gain and to live was Christ. He found that he did have a reason for living.

Yes, life was totally different for Grandpa now that he was applying Godly principles to his life and having fellowship with Him. I pray that you, too, will find God and have fellowship with Him. God knows where you are. He knows of your pain and sees your confusion. He wants to help you, but sin which brings pain and shame also separates us from God. But because of His love for you, you can have forgiveness of sins and have fellowship with Him through His son Jesus Christ.

If you feel you do not know God the way you should, and if you can't overcome sinful habits and your life is in a mess, don't give up. There is hope and there is a way. But its not the way of man, for his ways lead to destruction and last only for the short life we have here on earth. However, God's ways are higher and lead to a supreme life here on earth as well as in the life to come.

There are seven basic steps you can go through in finding God.

1. Discovery of sin—Hey, I'm a sinner and sin displeases God.

2. Be sorry for sins—I'm sorry for causing God great pain and exposing myself to punishment because of sin.

3. Confession of sins—God, I acknowledge my sins before You. I have no excuse for them.

4. Putting away sin—I renounce and give up my sinful ways and I won't go back to them again.

Courting and Married Life

5. Ask forgiveness for sin—God, I humble myself and ask You to forgive me and have mercy on me.

6. Consecration—I will serve You with all of my heart and will do all that I can for Your glory the rest of my life.

7. Faith in Jesus—Believe that Jesus Christ, God's son, died in your place, bearing your sins in His own body on the cross, and that He rose from the dead with resurrection power for you and me. Accept Him in your heart as your savior from sin.

(See John 3:16; Romans 3:23, 6:23, 10:9; Isaiah 53; Revelations 3:20.)

Always remember that if you do happen to slip and sin, God will forgive you.

Grandpa's conversion was the most important and valuable thing that ever happened to him. Needless to say, his whole outlook on life changed. He saw life in reality; he was no longer blinded and deceived. He grew stronger spiritually as he daily studied God's word and had fellowship with Him.

One thing in his life that changed because of his conversion was his idea about dating. No longer did he date for selfish reasons. He centered his relationships on Christ. When he dated he went to such

Courting and Married Life

activities as wholesome movies and church outings. He also prayed and read the Bible with the girls he dated. By doing this both he and his dates grew spiritually. Their relationship was stronger because it was centered on Christ, and not on her or him or sex or wealth. A marriage with the love of God will last.

He was glad he found the Lord before he found his mate. Now, with the guidance of the Lord, he could make a quality decision in finding a mate. Yes, he looked for a girl with outward beauty, but that wasn't the most important quality that he was searching for. What he really looked for was inward beauty, for he realized that down the road the outward beauty would fade.

One problem that he overcame after becoming a Christian was the nasty habit of smoking. That habit had gripped his life and was choking it out. One day as he was working in the garden, he looked at his cigarette and said, "What am I doing letting this weed control me?" He threw it away and didn't smoke again.

As a young Christian he became involved in prayer meetings, in singing in quartets, and in helping others. He made himself available and God began to use him. He would go to prayer meetings as often as he could, and would share things there that he had learned about his walk with God. In addition to singing in quartets, he would sing when doing his chores and while working throughout the day. Yes, his heart was happy for he had plenty to sing about. He would assist others when they needed extra help in mending fences, rounding up cows, building a home, etc. Yes, he enjoyed giving of himself and of his time to others, for God had placed a love in his heart for others.

As he gave himself to God, he continued to be blessed for years to come. One of his biggest blessings was finding the wife of his youth. Now that Grandpa had the first and most important priority in life established, that of his personal, intimate relationship with God, he was ready for the second, a personal, intimate relationship with his mate.

The Wife of His Youth

One thing for sure, every young man has his eyes peeled and is always looking for the wife of his youth. He is looking for a girl with great beauty, a girl with good personality and character; a girl to whom he can relate; a girl who can help him and be a blessing instead of a burden in times of adversity and weakness; a girl whom he can love and cherish and hold dear to his heart; one to whom he can be a comfort and a strength. But he must realize that just as he is not perfect, there is no perfect girl.

I asked Grandpa and others who have had successful marriages what they would look for in a girl. First of all they said they would ask if she had a good relationship with God. Did she love the Lord with all her heart? Second, they would ask her how her mother treated her husband. Finally, they would ask her how she related and submitted to her parents. I think this is pretty sound advice for young men who want a young girl who will be a blessing and not a curse to them all the days of their lives.

Grandpa finally met a girl with these qualities. His heart jumped for joy, for she was a beautiful young lady with long black hair, and she loved the Lord with all her heart. Her name was Alice Urna Singletary, a school teacher who was a few years younger than him. He had grown up with Alice but did not notice her until he started getting more involved at church. There he observed her at singings and revivals and other church events. It was evident that she really loved the Lord, for she sang with great joy and talked about Jesus with enthusiasm. Yet, he realized that God was still changing things in her life just as He was in his.

Finally, Grandpa asked Alice out to a church picnic. He really enjoyed her fellowship throughout the day as they played games and talked about the Lord. He began to admire Alice's beauty and saw that he could really relate to her. He said to himself, "Wow man! She is all right!" He decided that day that he would pursue her and get to know her better. As they dated, his love for her grew steadily.

Courting and Married Life

Grandpa began seeing Alice quite often. Almost every evening he was over at her house, courting her. He wished that he could be with her all the time, for she was such an inspiration and blessing to him. Finally, he decided in his heart that she was the one for him and that he must ask her to marry him.

Grandpa dressed rather nicely on the evening that he planned to propose. He was filled with excitement and wonder as he put on some cologne. He walked down the familiar trail to Alice's house, his heart thumped loudly as he drew closer. He picked some flowers for her on his way, and they sat on the porch and watched the sun go down. They talked about various things as Grandpa tried to figure out how to propose to her. She sensed that he was nervous about something and asked what was wrong. He said, "Oh, nothing. Nothing's wrong." She said, "Well, what's bothering you?" He said, "I just have something I need to ask you." She looked at him with a twinkle in her eyes and with expectation. He said, "You know we've been seeing each other quite a bit and I really love you a lot and I'd like to spend the rest of my life with you. What I want to ask you is, will you marry me?" A big smile came over her face, and with great joy in her heart, she said, "I love you very much and I would love to marry you."

Grandpa's heart was relieved to hear those words. He went away that night rejoicing, for he would be married soon. His thoughts became

Courting and Married Life

rather sobering, since he realized the responsibility that he was taking on. To whom much is given, much is required. He knew he would have to provide his wife with a home, food, clothes, love, understanding and tender care. Then, of course, they would have children, and he would be responsible for clothing, sheltering and raising them in the admonition and love of the Lord, training them and teaching them Godly principles. He was facing a great responsibility, but when he counted the cost he decided he was ready to jump over the broom stick. (Grandpa said back then they jumped over a broomstick when they got married. One day he asked with a chuckle, "I wonder if they jumped back over the broomstick when they are divorced.")

Their marriage would be a secret between them and God. They decided to get married by a Justice of the Peace since they didn't have much money. A day was chosen to go to Donaldsonsville, which was at one time the capitol of Louisiana. When Grandpa was married, they didn't have a big shindig like they do nowadays. He just got up that morning and went out to the barn and hooked up his dad's horse and buggy. After that he went back inside and put on some nice clothes. He didn't even own a suit then and he surely wouldn't have rented one even if he could have. He climbed into the carriage and headed for his girlfriend's. When he saw her, his thoughts of his awesome responsibility

Courting and Married Life

faded away. As they say nowadays, "she was a righteous fox", and he loved her.

Grandpa and Grandma took the ferry across the mighty Mississippi River to Donsonville to the Justice of Peace, where they were married on May 17, 1917.

The starry eyed couple had no trouble finding the courthouse because it was a well-known land mark with a convenient hitching-post in front. The horse was hitched on the outside while his owner and companion were there to get hitched on the inside. After climbing the front steps, they approached a clerk who was seated behind a desk. When he saw the couple, he broke into a grin. "What can I do for you?" he wanted to know, not needing to ask, for he was accustomed to the signs of lovers and their intentions. Grandpa spoke up, "We've come to get married." After asking their ages, (Grandpa was twenty-six and Alice was twenty-four), a license was issued, with no waiting period required. A judge sat daily in the courthouse, and uniting couples was foremost on his agenda. (Divorce was unheard of then in that area of the country.) With a twinkle in his eye, he said, "All you need is two witnesses," so Grandpa went outside and found two men standing nearby who were thrilled to assist the judge in legal matters. The couple was pronounced man and wife before ten minutes had expired on the big town clock, Mr. and Mrs. William

Courting and Married Life

Thomas Williams emerged from the front entrance into a lifetime together, bonded by their love and commitment to each other. Grandpa assisted his new bride into the waiting carriage for the ride into the unknown future. In about two hours, they arrived at the home of her married sister and his married brother. Two sisters had now married two brothers, and family ties were now greatly bonded. After much jubilation, "Why didn't you let us in on it," the first-marrieds accepted the newlyweds, and gave them their blessings. Both sets of parents gave theirs, also. The sun was beginning to sink in the western sky and the first day until death would dissolve the union was coming to an end. They then went to what would be their home for the next year, a small house on his dad's place.

Getting Started

Grandpa realized that getting started was going to be tough. He was going to need money to get his own place established. About a year after they were married he was drafted into the army. Before he left, their first born, Adrian Delton, was born. Eight days later Grandpa had to leave for boot camp. He hated to leave his wife and son, but duty called.

Grandpa was first stationed at Alexandria, Louisiana. When he arrived he soon found out why it was called boot camp. The young soldiers got

Courting and Married Life

booted around a lot there. That was really rough on Grandpa, and his heart longed to be back home with his wife and son.

From Alexandria he was transferred to Kentucky where he was to receive his final training before going overseas to fight in a cruel, bloody war. However, just a day before his unit was to be sent overseas, Grandpa and his tentmates were quarantined with measles. The rest of the unit went overseas, and it's members were shot up pretty badly.

Grandpa knew that God was keeping him from harm, and that He had a purpose for his life. Grandma also knew that God was working on their behalf. She had been praying day and night for her husband. She was a righteous woman, and God gave her the desires of her heart.

Grandpa remained in Kentucky, where he was discharged at the end of the war. He served in the army for about nine months, but that was plenty long enough for him. Upon his discharge he went home as quickly as possible because his beautiful wife and son were waiting for him. He greeted them with great love and thanked God for reuniting them. His son cried, for he did not know this stranger. However, in no time the boy learned that this man really loved him, and he felt very secure around his father.

One of the first things that Grandpa did when he returned home was to buy some land and begin

Courting and Married Life

building a house on it. He bought twenty acres of land for twenty dollars an acre, land that was connected to nine acres that he had bought before going into the service. He rented a house for two dollars and fifty cents a month while he built his own. He didn't want to owe money for the rest of his life, so he saved and did without while he was young so that he could have his own place. Later in life he inherited more land.

During the time that he was getting his farm established, he worked on several different jobs so that he could pay for farm equipment, doctor bills and new-coming babies. For a period he worked at a saw mill located in the Mackeroy Swamp in Garyville, Louisiana. This was hard work, but he wanted to provide for his family and get a farm started. When spring came he quit the job so that he could plant his spring crop.

He also worked for a time as a guard, guarding convicts working on the Mississippi River levee. This was an unpleasant job, and he saw some nasty things happen there. For instance, one time a captain saw a convict do something that he didn't like, so he ordered four men to pull down the convict's pants and hold him on the ground while he beat him with a whip. Grandpa didn't like seeing things like that, but he continued working there for six months so that he could accomplish his goals.

Grandpa was on duty one time when the Mississippi River was extremely high. Men on each side of the river were standing guard to keep anyone from blowing a hole in the levee and flooding the river banks. One night a small boat approached their side of the river. Grandpa and his friends shouted for the occupants to stop, but they kept coming. The guards opened fire on them because they wouldn't identify themselves or their intentions. Grandpa said he thinks they were killed.

Grandpa gradually increased the amount of farm equipment, cattle and other livestock that he owned, and he fixed up his house and bought some luxuries for his wife. He bought such things as a new scrub board, pots and pans, and even a new dress and a dresser to go with it. Finally, he got himself situated so that he could live off of the produce of his farm.

During this time he was blessed with many sons and daughters.

The Fruit of the Womb

The fruit of the womb-how blessed are they who have children. What an awesome responsibility it is. Children are the future of the nation. They will either be a blessing or a curse to those around them. What a responsibility to train up a child in the way he should go. It takes time, care, understanding and love, and begins even in the mother's womb. In a very special God-given way, the mother cares and provides for the child within her as it develops and

Courting and Married Life

Courting and Married Life

strengthens and prepares for its entry into the world.

Raising children is quite a task, and shouldn't be taken lightly, for parents are responsible to provide for their children spiritually, physically and mentally. Grandpa and Grandma were mature adults, yet there were many things they had to learn when they started having children. They sought advice from their parents and friends who had had children before. They also sought God for instruction on raising their children. Through the next few pages I will give you a brief history of all of their children. I believe their parents did a good job in raising them.

The first-born child was Adrian Delton, born June 14, 1918. When he was a young man he left home and joined the navy. Everyone knew of the danger that lay ahead of him, yet he served willingly. He fought and died so that his country would remain free. He was killed on December 7, 1941 in the bombing of Pearl Harbor, one of the many men who went down on the battleship Arizona.

Their second-born was a girl, born February 3, 1920. She would be their only daughter and was named Birma Rama. She grew to be a very beautiful girl. Grandpa said there were guys from all over the country hanging around the house courting her. Having eight brothers, she learned to work hard and love others. Her mother, a Godly woman who

Courting and Married Life

lived what she taught, spent a lot of time with her and I believe that she learned a lot of Godly traits from her. I pray that you are living the Godly principles that you should be teaching. You are teaching Godly principles, aren't you?

Aunt Birma was married on June 14, 1941 to Mc Vea Boze. They had one son. She was married a second time to Charles Montet on January 15, 1950. That marriage produced four daughters and one son.

The third-born child was Dwight Lincoln. He was born on October 8, 1921 and he grew to be a man who loved and served the Lord with all his heart. He had a very successful career in the navy as an airplane pilot, and retired as a high ranking officer.

During his early years in the service Dwight had a once-in-a-lifetime experience. The ship that he was on, the Battleship Missouri, was selected to carry President Truman and his family from Brazil back to the States. One day President Truman was playing the piano, and his daughter Margaret was singing for the crew. She didn't want to sing alone, so she tried to get some of the officers to sing with her. They were dumbfounded and bashful, and did not know what to do, so they refused the invitation. However, Uncle Dwight, coming from a singing family said he would love to sing. Everyone looked at him as if he were crazy. He sang with the

President's daughter while the President played the piano. He really enjoyed singing with them and he realized that they were human beings just like him.

Later, Dwight married Barbara Young on June 21, 1947. They lived in Georgia, and had three sons and one daughter. He also became president of the Gideons in the state of Georgia. (The Gideons is an organization of businessmen that distributes Bibles around the world.)

The fourth-born was Jennings Bryan, born on April 28, 1923. He grew up to be a missionary in Brazil. Before going to the mission field he met a young lady named Sara Schlaback. They attended Bible college together, and were married on August 29, 1947. His wife was a hard-working woman, faithfully committed to her husband and his work. They had eleven children, four girls and seven boys. Some were born in Brazil and some here in America. One of their oldest sons, David, died as an infant in Brazil. They led a vigorous life, conforming to the lifestyle of a people of a foreign nation. The Lord called them to do a special work to share the gospel of Christ. They counted it a joy and a blessing to be in service for Him.

Uncle Bryan's service to the Lord was costly, for not only did he lose a son on the mission field, but he also lost his wife. When she was around fifty she became quite ill. Deep in the Amazon jungles the

Courting and Married Life

medical facilities and technology weren't very good. Shortly after they got her to a hospital she passed on to be with the Lord, her savior, redeemer, and creator. Because she remembered her creator in her youth, she now lives for eternity with Him in heaven.

Uncle Bryan returned to America where he still lives. He remarried Ruby Galman, who, like him, seeks to do good for the kingdom of God. He likes to sing praises to God, preach and play the guitar for the Lord.

The years went by, and another son, Benson Capper, was born on December 31, 1924. On February 11, 1947, shortly after he was discharged from the navy, he was walking with his girlfriend on the streets of California. As they walked, quietly enjoying the fresh air, and discussing plans for their future, they heard a car coming screeching around a corner. Capper alertly pushed his girlfriend to the side. The car ran over him, crushing his life and future out of his hands. His friend was also hit, but she survived. I pray that Capper had treasures laid up in heaven, and that you do also, for this night your soul could be required of you. Then whose shall those things be which thou hast provided? (See Luke 12:16-21.)

The sixth-born child was Holmes Thurman, born on March 3, 1927. Holmes suffered from spinal meningitis, which left him with a curved spine. One time when his doctor was out of town, other doctor gave him some improper medicine which caused a blood clot. Holmes died as a result of that clot. Holmes had a humped back, and I'm sure many of the kids made fun of him as he grew up, but he did not let that keep God from developing him into a beautiful, intelligent, loving and happy human being. He let God develop his inner man, for he knew the inner quality of life effected the outer aspects.

Holmes worked for the state of Louisiana, and had several workers under him. Everyone loved and appreciated him, for he was full of love and understanding. The Lord also loved him and took him home to be with Him on July 28, 1963. Now Uncle Holmes has a perfect body and lives in an eternal home where there is no criticism, mockery or hatred, but where there is plenty of love.

Holmes left his dad an insurance inheritance of ten thousand dollars and fifteen acres of land. Grandpa gave it all to his children.

Ira Hilton was born on December 23, 1928. He is a very gentle and patient man who loves the Lord with all of his heart. He shares this love with everyone, reaching out to let the world around him know that God loves them, also. He married Ann Gree on March 1, 1952. They had six children, four girls and two sons. He worked as a telephone repairmen and is now retired. He also sings, preaches and plays the harmonica.

Uncle Hilton made it a habit to regularly visit Grandpa in his old age. He would help him bathe and get ready for church on Sunday mornings and Wednesday evenings. He did many things for his dad, because he loved him.

I have noticed that all of Grandpa's children reached out, loved, and helped him in his later years. I can only believe that this is because Grandpa loved and reached out to them throughout his life. I hope that you are loving and reaching out to your children the way God would have you to.

The eighth-born child was Shelby Keelan, born on November 21, 1930. He grew up to be a hard working man. He married Peggy Lorraine Davis on December 19, 1953, and they had three boys and two girls. Shelby and Peggy were my parents.

Dad worked hard most of his life (as an industrial insulator) to keep his family fed, clothed and sheltered. From time to time he went about preaching and singing about the love of God. He taught his children to preach and sing about the love of God, also. One time as part of his ministry, he made a full-play album with gospel music on it.

He is now enjoying the benefits of retirement. God has used him in many ways and I know He will continue using him. He will also use you if you let

Courting and Married Life

Him, but first you must have peace and harmony with yourself and those around you. There will be no peace until God is seated at the conference table on the throne of your heart. Then he will use you and lead you to peace and happiness.

Last, but not least, the baby of the family was born on September 6, 1932. His name is Gyles Zimri, now nicknamed Zack. He has many friends, for he shows himself friendly. He is a very easygoing man. He was married on June 26, 1954 to Rita Mae Laiche, and they had five children—one good looking son and four beautiful daughters. Gyles is respected and liked by young and old alike because he is still young in heart and has the love of Jesus in him. He was active in various sports most of his life, and still participates from time to time, even though he is in his fifties. He also plays the piano and sings for the glory of God. He is involved in various services to the church which he attends—teaching Sunday school, being an elder, and playing piano for song service. Gyles is now retired and leads a quiet and peaceful life, staying busy keeping his land and helping others.

Grandpa and Grandma raised some fine children who, through their service to the Lord, played an important role in making the world around them happier. Parents must be in agreement in serving the Lord. If they aren't there is conflict in the family, for more than one standard is expected of the children. Then the children's eyes cannot be single because there is more than one idea and standard coming from the parents. (See Matthew 6:22, Luke 11:34.) If your eye is not single, you cannot please the Lord, just as a house divided against itself will fall. There will be no peace in the family where this type of atmosphere is produced.

Grandpa and Grandma learned to seek to please Christ and not themselves. They learned that if they seek first the kingdom of God and His righteousness, they would obtain a peace and joy that the world doesn't give and the world can't take away. Remember, there will never be any peace until God is seated at the conference table (the throne) of your heart. Outward problems stem from inward problems, Refusing to dedicate personal rights and possessions to God leads to destruction of the total man.

I must say the fruit of the womb is something to cherish, and it is a big responsibility, for the way in which you live your life and train your children will determine much of their success and happiness in life. I pray you will do a good job.

The Loss of a Loved One

I'm sure it was rough on my grandparents as they watched seven of their sons serve in the navy at the same time. They kept their peace even though their first-born was killed in Pearl Harbor,

Courting and Married Life

another died on the streets of California, and yet another died of disease. You may ask how they kept their peace in the midst of tragedy. Well, it was because they kept their trust and faith in God. They held onto the God of their salvation instead of onto the world and its philosophies. They kept serving and pleasing Him through the good times and the bad times.

Because of their service to God, my grandparents had a very happy and successful marriage. Grandpa's farm was prosperous and his needs were met. One of the reasons Grandpa was prosperous was because he was a diligent worker, and not a slothful one.

Grandma was also a diligent worker, highly respected by her children and the community. You could compare her to the woman described in chapter thirty-one of Proverbs. Her commitment to and love of God was truly a blessing to her husband. A Godly woman plays an important part in the success of her husband.

Who can find a virtuous woman? Yes, her price is far above rubies. The heart of her husband doth safely trust in her, so that he shall have no need of spoil. She will do him good and not evil all the days of her life. Favor is deceitful and beauty is vain, but a woman that feareth the Lord, she shall be praised. (See Proverbs 31.)

Courting and Married Life

Grandma made and hand-washed a lot of their clothes. She also helped with a lot of the work around the farm, and helped teach her children educational, moral, and Godly principles and standards.

Grandpa was truly blessed with her. They didn't let conflicts separate them; instead, they let conflicts draw them closer, for they humbly sought the Lord's guidance and correction.

My grandparents' relationship improved as they grew older. Eventually their children were all grown and married. Grandpa allowed several of them to live at home for a short time after they were married, because he loved them and wanted to help them get established in their new roles in life.

Well, before long there were grandchildren everywhere, and these children brought a new zeal and a new meaning to my grandparents' lives. In raising their own children, they learned to be patient, gentle, understanding and firm, which gave them a lot more wisdom in handling their grandchildren and great-grandchildren. They really enjoyed that special blessing.

The years quickly passed, and it soon came time for Grandma to go home to be with her heavenly Father. As Grandpa said, "There's one thing for sure in life; you gonna die." Grandma passed away

Courting and Married Life

October 18, 1964 at the age of 71. She suffered from female problems the last few years of her life, as well as a tumor in her stomach which caused much pain. Through all this she managed to show kindness, joy and peace without being bitter, for her hope was built on nothing less than Jesus' love and righteousness.

Truly Grandma's death was a sorrowful event for Grandpa and the whole family. The woman that he had loved and cherished was gone, never to be seen again in this present world. Never again would her children feel her special way of loving them. Never again would he feel her gentle touch or have fellowship with her. Grandpa's heart was sad, but it also rejoiced, for he knew she was in heaven with her heavenly Father.

Surely the relationship that Grandpa had with God eased the pain of losing his companion of forty-seven years. He knew that Christ was still with him, and would continue to be, for He promised He would never leave nor forsake him. Because of this promise Grandpa was able to carry on in life because of the strength he had in Christ. His life was not totally based upon his wife, but on Christ. Therefore, his world did not fall apart.

Several years later Grandpa married Evie Michael Wall, whose husband had passed away. She lived across the street from Grandpa and was

Courting and Married Life

one of his childhood sweethearts (or he was one of hers). Whatever the case, they kind of liked each other when they were real young, but it never worked out. Since they had both lost a mate and were alone, they decided to get together and have some companionship in their later years. Age soon caught up with them, however, and Grandpa was very heartbroken, for within one year his second wife died.

After Grandpa lost his second wife, he decided that he would never remarry, even though there was one more lady who seemed to be interested in him. Mrs. Gonzales started sitting near him at church at just about every service. He was around ninety at the time and she was around eighty-three. A lot of people said she was making a move on him. Whether she was making a move or just looking for a friend more her age, I really don't know, but I do know that Grandpa did not make a move on her. They sat together as friends until Grandpa died.

One time Grandpa wore a medal to church that he had received during the war. As he was showing it to Mrs. Gonzales, it fell to the floor. When Mrs. Gonzales picked it up, he got upset with her, because he didn't want her to think that he was giving it to her. He didn't want her to get the wrong impression. Grandpa got his medal back real quick-like.

Courting and Married Life

Before we move on to the next chapter I would like to say a few things about Grandpa's marriages, both of which were happy and successful, lasting until death took his mates. It makes you wonder what the keys to his successful marriges were, in a country where over fifty percent of all marriages end up in divorce.

His marriages were built on a sure foundation, the principles of God who created man and woman and who ordained marriage. He wasn't a selfish person; he loved his mate the same as he loved himself, for they were one in marriage. Finally, he was patient, kind, understanding, long-suffering, humble, etc. (The characteristics of love are found in I Corinthians 13:4-7.)

It has been found that couples who pray and study God's word together have successful marriages. If you are single and dating, you and your friend ought to make it a habit to study God's word and pray together. If you continue this practice after you are married, you will be basing your relationship on God, who is the sure foundation for any marriage.

If you're married and you're not now doing this, you and your spouse need to start seeking the Lord together with a humble heart and open ears. Through this seeking the Lord can lead and guide you into an abundant life and successful marriage.

"He hath shown thee, O man, what is good; and what doth the LORD require of thee, but to do justly, and to love mercy, and to walk humbly with thy God." (Micah 6:8, KJV)

Chapter 4

Later Generation Activities

Just to show you how interests are passed down from generation to generation, I will share with you a few examples of the activities of Grandpa's children and grandchildren. They also played games on Sunday evenings after church, and some times they got involved too much.

One time while playing football, Grandpa's son Gyles somehow got thrown into a fencepost and broke his arm while trying to tackle his cousin. On another occasion a bunch of cousins got together and had a sling shot war, shooting dirt clogs at each other and having a good old time. However, their

Later Generation Activities

fun suddenly came to a halt as Shelby, hiding in the loft of the barn, was shot by a cousin. The cousin who was running by jumped up and without thinking shot him. Shelby was hit in the eye, and went to yelling and screaming. That brought the little war to an end. His cousin's problem was that he didn't think before he acted. He didn't know where he would hit his target. We, too, often act without thinking, and later regret our actions.

The victim was taken to a doctor who sent him to a specialist in New Orleans. The specialist said that he didn't think the boy would ever be able to see out of the eye again. However, his parents believed God could restore his eye and in several days he began to regain his vision. In time the eye healed.

Later in the day of the accident, the sheriff came by and talked to Grandpa because he had heard that his son had been shot by a black man. In those days many people called a slingshot a "nigger shooter", and by the time the sheriff had heard about the accident the story was twisted. That's why we should be sure to get the message clear when someone talks to us. We can cause a lot of damage to people's lives by misunderstanding and misinterpreting stories that we hear.

Another time Grandpa's sons were throwing darts. Each dart consisted of a piece of wood with

Later Generation Activities

nails driven through it. Gyles attempted to pull a dart from the board as someone threw a dart. It hit him on the back of the head, and he began screaming and running. When his brothers finally caught him, they found a nail stuck in the back of his head. Gyles had to be held down as the nail was pulled out. Blood gushed everywhere. The bleeding finally stopped, and eventually the injury healed. From this I hope that you see that we need to be more careful of our actions.

My cousins and I (representing the next generation) also got together for group activities. One day we got into a potato fight and my older brother Shelby became a victim of a flying potato. As we threw potatoes at each other without thinking of what could happen, he was hit in the eye. Although he wasn't injured seriously, it did hurt for a while, and it ended our potato fight.

One time a bunch of us got together to play some tackle football. One of my cousins was running the ball; and as I came from behind to tackle him, someone else approached from the front. We were both running full blast, but from opposite directions. We put our heads on the same side of the ball carrier's waist to tackle him. Pow! We hit head on without the protection of helmets or pads. Both of the tacklers fell to the ground and the ball carrier kept running for a touchdown. I saw stars, and my injured cousin ran off to put cold water on his head.

Later Generation Activities

When I got up blood, started gushing out of my head. I thought it was sweat until I wiped my head and saw the blood. Everyone told me to lie on my back so that the blood wouldn't come out so fast. I was taken to a doctor and he shaved off my eyebrow and put seven stitches above my right eye.

One time my brother Shelby and cousin Randy were racing and catching wheelies on a riding lawn mower. The lawn mower had a rapidly turning open sprocket beneath the seat. Shelby would get behind the lawn mower and pull down on the seat while Randy released the clutch to catch the wheelie. One time Randy stood up while Shelby was pulling down on the seat. Randy sat back down to an unpleasant surprise, as he landed on an open sprocket instead of the seat. Was he surprised! Everyone started hollering, and his mom came running. Randy ran toward her saying, "It's just a little hole, Momma, don't whip me. I didn't mean to do it. It's a little hole." I guess he was worried about the hole in his pants. His parents couldn't whip him for quite some time because he had around three hundred stitches in his behind.

As we can see through these stories, children who are left to themselves and who don't follow instructions can end up in a lot of trouble. Of course, a lot of times we grownups leave chldren alone and don't give them proper instructions or sound reasoning. If children get into trouble under these

Later Generation Activities

circumstances, the adults are at fault, and not the children.

In the Christian walk, Christ said He would never leave us nor forsake us. We have the word of God as an instruction manual for life. If we would use it we would avoid a lot of problems. When we make mistakes and get into trouble, it's our fault. God has given us all the instructions and comfort we need for our walk through life. When we do make mistakes He will forgive us if we ask, and he will lead us in the right way. That's why we must not lean on our own understanding, but acknowledge him in all our ways. If we do this, He will guide us into paths that lead to a peaceful, joyous, victorious lives. (See Proverbs 3:5, 6.)

Chapter Five

Old But Still Active

The Decaying, Yet Renewed Man

Grandpa began feeling his physical strength leave as his body grew older and began decaying. He lost his teeth and had to get false ones. His eyes became weak and he began to wear glasses. He started losing his hearing. His body began moving slowly and he began using a cane. He also had to stop driving.

Yet, despite all those body losses he was still happy and active. He kept on keeping on, and that's what you must do to succeed in life. In spite of his old body, he was still happy and youthful in his

Old But Still Active

spirit. Your spirit lives forever. Your body will get old and die, but your inner man will live forever. That's why Grandpa was happy and cheerful and useful in his old age. He took care of his inner man. He fed it good spiritual food, the word of God. He gave it fellowship with God and his people. He kept it clean by repenting of his wrong doing, by asking Jesus to forgive him, and by standing and doing what was right in the sight of God.

Instead of being bitter, inactive and unpleasant in his old age, Grandpa was happy, active and very pleasant to be around. I remember how he would always whistle while working in the garden. He counted it a blessing to be able to work.

From time to time something would happen and he wouldn't be able to whistle, sometimes for months. I don't know whether or not this had something to do with his old age, but it didn't discourage him. He would just sing and hum more. I think this is one of the reasons why he lived so long. After all, the Bible does say that a merry heart is like a medicine, and he had a very merry heart.

One of the reasons that Grandpa had a merry heart was because he didn't have the burden of sin upon him. He accepted the fact that Jesus had died so that he could be forgiven of his sins and be restored to a right relationship with God. Accepting this, he also forgave himself, being set free from the bondage and burden of sin. I have heard it said that

Old But Still Active

over fifty percent of the people in mental hospitals could go home immediately if they could forgive themselves and forget the past. If you can't forgive yourself, how can you forgive others?

Day to Day Life

Even though Grandpa was old, he stayed very busy. He would usually get up and go to bed with the chickens. I remember him telling me that the younger generation is like an animal-they sleep during the day and come out at night.

When he got up, he did so slowly, but surely. As he moved around and got his blood circulating, he would head for the stove. After a good cup of coffee he would put on his clothes and put in his teeth. Next, he would put on his glasses, find his boots, and put them on. He would then find one of his hats and put it on. Usually in the summer he wore his African safari hat to keep the sun off of his face and head. During the winter he wore his wool insulated hats to keep his ears warm.

After he was all dressed, whether it be winter or summer, rain or shine, he would head out the back door, down the steps and across the pasture to the chicken pen. There were many animals in the chicken pen—ducks, goats, turkeys, calves and, of course, chickens. The animals would anxiously await his arrival, for they knew that he fed them.

Old But Still Active

The turkey would sometimes chase people, the goat would eat everything in sight, and the ducks would make mud holes. However, he had more problems with chickens than anything else. Some of them would get out and wait around the house for him to come and feed them. They would run around, eat in the pasture, and lay eggs all over the countryside.

Grandpa's garden was a favorite target for the chickens. Grandpa kept his eye on them, and if they got too close to the garden he would whoop and yell, and they would head back to their pen. Before long he would catch them back in the garden again. Sometimes he threw his cane at them. He blamed the roosters for leading the hens to the garden. One day he got tired of it, and he got several young guys together and told them they could have the roosters if they caught and killed them. Grandpa stood back and chuckled as he watched four or five young guys chase the roosters all over his place. They killed the ones Grandpa wanted killed and took them home for supper. That kept the chickens out of the garden for a while, but before long they were back again. Grandpa hooped and hollered and threw his cane at them once more. After a few weeks he was again tired of chasing the roosters. There was one old rooster that they didn't get the first time, and Grandpa blamed him for the trouble. He got out his shotgun, shot the rooster, and gave it to a neighbor.

Old But Still Active

Well, he had a time with those chickens until he died.

When he was through tending to the chickens he would work in his garden for two or three hours. He really liked working in the garden, and at harvest time you could tell that he had spent many hours there, for he had some beautiful crops. He constantly worked to keep the weeds out of it and to keep it properly cultivated and watered. The same should apply to us. We should work hard to keep our lives cultivated and watered with the word and Spirit of God in order to keep out the weeds and decay of sin.

Grandpa didn't raise his produce to feast on himself, for he ate very little from his gardens. He gave away just about everything he grew. If he didn't give his produce to relatives or to his friends at church, he would get someone to take it to the poor and needy. In his earlier years Grandpa had planted several pecan, pear and fig trees, and every year he gave away bag after bag of fruit from these trees. He not only gave, but he gave cheerfully. God loves a cheerful giver.

Grandpa didn't like to waste. Once he stumbled and fell in the pasture. As he lay there face down, struggling to get up, he noticed a fence about twenty yards away. He crawled toward it, and while doing so, he came upon a pecan lying on the ground. (Here he is in a fix and he's not the least bit worried.) He calmly picked up the pecan and stuck it in his pocket. With renewed strength and vigor he struggled even harder until finally he was at the fence. He used it to pull himself to his feet.

He was diligent in his work, and toiled through the heat of the summer and the cold of the winter, in the rain and in the mud. One cold, rainy and muddy day, as he was working in the garden, his boots sank into the mud and he was stuck there. As he struggled to free himself, he fell over in the mud. There was no one around to help him, and he thought to himself: "This is where I could end up." Here he was, 91 years old, lying stuck in the mud. But did he give up? No! He had been though many struggles before, and wasn't about to go out without a fight. He finally pulled himself to a standing position and freed himself. Despite his age and weakness, he was still able to get himself out of the fix he had gotten himself into. If we could learn to keep struggling and fighting and to not give up, we, too, can get out of the many fixes we get ourselves into.

When Grandpa was through working in the garden, he would go back into the house and fix breakfast and drink more coffee. On many occasions he would find the coffee all burnt up because he had forgotten to turn it off when he went to work in the garden. After breakfast he would sit and prop up his feet by the space heater and read his paper and his Bible and pray. During the summer he sat on the porch and read, prayed and relaxed. After that he would take a nap for an hour or two. His supper would often consist of jambalaya, (which is a mixture of such things as spiced rice, onions, meat, and beans) or goulash. He was a good cook. He knew how to mix that stuff up real well. After getting it started, he would head out to the garden for an hour or two, making use of every spare moment. He would get carried away in the garden, and several times he forgot that he had food cooking, only to come in to some burnt food. It's a wonder the house never caught on fire. I believe the Lord was really watching over him.

After eating, he would head back out to work a little more, and to feed the animals before retiring for the day. I can still hear him coming in, whistling and singing. About dark he would come in, take off his clothes and glasses, and sink down into his bed. In no time he was sound asleep. Just think, he didn't even take sleeping pills or aspirin. He hardly ever used medicine or went to doctors, simply because he chose not to, even though he probably should have sometimes.

Well, that was his typical day in his old age, except on Sundays and Wednesdays.

A Church Goer

Grandpa loved to go to church and went as often as he could, usually on Sundays and Wednesdays.

Old But Still Active

Most of the time his Wednesdays were different from the other weekdays. He usually got up and did the same chores, but around 10 a.m. he would come in and clean up and get dressed. This was the day that his daughter, Birma, and her husband would come out to clean house. When they finished their work, they would take Grandpa shopping and out to eat. When Birma couldn't do Grandpa's cleaning, her daughter-in-law, Shony, would often take her place. I found both Birma and Shony to be very kind, compassionate, and hard-working ladies.

Grandpa looked forward to Wednesdays. It was a time for him to get out, to see some old friends and to gallivant around. Sometimes they would go to New Orleans and eat at a fancy restaurant, and sometimes they would eat in Gonzales at a McDonalds or a Burger King. Grandpa enjoyed going to those local restaurants, because there was usually someone there to whom he could talk. Boy, did he enjoy talking and joking around. He was continuously cutting little jokes or telling stories. As he got older his memory faded, and he began telling the same stories over and over. However, I still enjoyed hearing them.

Groceries were usually bought at Winn Dixie, a store located in a field where he used to raise cotton. As they shopped, Grandpa would strut up and down the aisles, talking to people as he went. He would buy such things as sausage, bread, corn flakes, and other small necessities. He loved bananas, and often bought them.

When the shopping was finished, the group would head back home. Aunt Birma and Uncle Charlie would drop Grandpa off and return to their home, also. Being tired from all the excitement, Grandpa would go right to bed for a nap. In an hour or so he would awaken, looking forward to going to church that night. After feeding the chickens he would eat a little dinner, shave and get ready for church. His son Gyles would pull up and toot his horn two or three times, and Grandpa would hurry to the front door, turn on the porch light, fasten the door, climb into the car and head out for church.

Grandpa loved to go to church. He went twice on Sundays and every Wednesday night, and any other time there was a service. At ninety-two years of age he was still going to church whenever the doors were open. He had seen much in his life, and he knew that going to church was good for him. Being with God's people would edify him and strengthen him, as they sang praises to God and heard His word.

He didn't go to church just to receive, he went to give as well. That's one of the reasons why I believe he enjoyed life so much. He had learned to give. He would give praise to God, give his tithes and offerings, and give and be a blessing to the people around him.

Old But Still Active

On his birthday he would usually sing a special song with his sons. He also sang in the church choir. It was really a blessing to the people to see a man of his age still singing and being active in the church. He was a blessing to the little children, as well. He would give them candy peppermints, and nickles or dimes or quarters. The children would gather around him waiting to be blessed. Grandpa really loved little children. I can still see him holding his great grandchildren, with a big smile of joy and pride on his face. It made him very happy to know that his seed would be carried on from generation to generation.

Sunday was Grandpa's day of rest. He would feed the chickens in the morning, go to church, and then come home and eat dinner. He usually ate his Sunday dinner next door with his son, Gyles. When he was through eating he would slowly walk home and take a nap or relax by the space heater or on the swing on the porch. He also like watching Hee Haw on Sunday afternoons. Later in the evening he would feed the chickens again, and head back to church for the night service. He had other activities to keep him occupied. He would sing with a group once a month at the old folk's home. Quite often he had children, grandchildren, or friends drop in to visit him. From time to time he would go out and get seed for his garden, or feed for his chickens. He also kept an eye out for his chickens, so that dogs, cats and hawks wouldn't get them. He would keep

Old But Still Active

his shotgun loaded. From time to time you could hear him shoot at a dog and pepper him. Boy, you could hear that dog yelping as it ran away from the chicken pen. One time he saw a hawk eyeing the chickens from a tree about three hundred and fifty feet away. He got his gun and went out to the side of the barn, took careful aim, and shot and killed that hawk.

As you can see, Grandpa was very active in his old age. He was very kind and considerate, and was an encouragement to his fellowman. I hope that if you're an older person that you are encouraged to be more active and useful and helpful despite any handicaps that you might have, for you still can be a blessing and encouragement to mankind. I pray that if you're young you will learn to respect, love, cherish and take heed to the elderly, for they have traveled many paths that you will travel someday.

Chapter Six

The Final Round

The Final Week at Home

Grandpa usually spent Christmas with his son, Gyles, but the Christmas of 1982 he chose to spend alone at his home. For several years he had been telling Gyles that he would spend his last Christmas alone. He had recently seen several visions of heaven and heard angels singing, which led him to believe that his time on earth was short.

In his long life he witnessed many inventions, such as television, cars, and other luxuries of today. His first car was a second-hand crank. It cost sixty dollars and it lasted a long time. He then bought a brand new Ford for five hundred dollars. His sons were glad he bought it because it brought a lot of

The Final Round

attention to them. All of their friends and neighbors came over and wanted to ride in it. It was just about the only car in that area. One day a bunch of his friends were out riding in it. There were so many people in it that some of them had to stand on the running board. They were riding around cutting up and having a good old time. Their fun came to an end when they started harassing some longhorn cows. The cows didn't think the car was so cool, and they attacked it and knocked one of the boys off the side. No one was hurt but they were frightened.

Grandpa saw many things and many people come and go in the ninety-two years that he lived here on earth. The life of William Thomas Williams, better known as Uncle Tom, or Grandpa, or PaPa was drawing to a close. The final round of his life was a struggle and a hard time for Grandpa and the family, for he was suffering from prostate problems and cancer. He had been ill for some time, but had kept it to himself. He never did like to go to doctors or to take medicine, and he didn't like imposing upon people, either.

Finally some of his children talked him into going to see the doctor who said he was in pretty bad shape, and gave him some medicine to help him with his prostrate problem.

The thing that was amazing was that Grandpa didn't show that he was ill. He was a very courageous man. He still worked in the garden and fed

The Final Round

his chickens just as much as before his illness. He continued to attend church and to sing in the choir, and was still cheerful, loving and giving of himself. He kept active up until two weeks before his death. As a matter of fact, on his last Sunday in church he eased up the steps to the stage and sang in the choir with all of his might. He loved to sing, and he sang with all of his heart. No one expected that this would be the last time they would see him in church alive, but Grandpa had only two weeks left here on earth.

The next morning Grandpa went to feed the chickens for the final time. Little did they know that this would be the last time that he would feed them. No longer would he be around to give them special care. After he died I believe they missed him, also.

After feeding his chickens, Grandpa completed his last trip through the pasture, walked into the house and went straight to bed. It was as if he had said as Paul did, My time has come, my life is finished. I am now ready to be offered up and the time of my departure is at hand. I have fought the good fight. I have finished my course. I have kept the faith. Henceforth there is laid up for me a crown of righteousness. (See II Timothy 6-8.) The next day as I stood in his room and looked at him with concern and worry, he looked up at me, and with a weak chuckle, said, "Boy, you don't know what's a-coming do you?" Yes, he knew it was his time.

The Final Round

Grandpa grew weaker and sicker, and was finally confined to bed. His children tried to comfort and nurse him. They would bathe him, feed him and give him his medicine, hoping and praying that he would snap out of it, as he did many other times when he was sick. Before he would just fight off his illness and keep on going, but this time it was as if he said, "Well, its my time, so why fight it." He grew gradually weaker and one week later, on a Sunday night, they put him in the hospital.

A Week of Pain

The doctors said Grandpa was in critical condition and they could not tell how much longer he would live. They started feeding him through his veins and giving him oxygen through a plastic hose in his nose. He didn't like this at all. I guess he thought, "Can't a man die in peace?" By this time someone from the family was with him twenty-four hours around the clock. His lips and tongue became very chapped for he had to breath through his mouth because of the oxygen hoses stuck in his nose. He also got saliva in his throat, making it hard to breathe. The saliva had to be removed with a suction hose.

Because of his prostrate problems, special provisions had to be made for him to go to the bathroom, and he was in a lot of pain over this condition.

Even though Grandpa was heavily medicated, half out of his mind with pain, and on the verge of

The Final Round

death, from time to time he would start whistling, humming, or singing an old hymn right there on his deathbed. Yes, he still had peace in his heart and an assurance that he was going to be with his heavenly Father.

For several days there was a hush over the hospital room, for it was evident that death coming. Many of Grandpa's relatives and children stayed with him that last week. They would quietly try to comfort him in any way that they could, hoping and praying that he would pull through. You could sense that his long, cheerful and prosperous life was coming to an end quickly. Never more would he roam and toil in the fields of this earth, for death was moving upon him quickly.

By this time Grandpa had been in the hospital a week. He was restless and not sleeping much, a result of being in a strange environment with tubes up his nose and other contraptions all around him. He stopped breathing hard about four on Monday morning and gently went to sleep. It was the first time he had slept well since he had been admitted to the hospital. His youngest son Gyles and his wife Rita Mae was staying with him at the time. They were relieved to see him sleeping soundly.

The day before, a Sunday, everyone had been praying that Grandpa would snap out of it. As I talked with different people that day, it seemed that we all had the same attitude of prayer. We

The Final Round

asked that the Lord would either heal him quickly or take him home quickly, for it hurt us to see him go through such pain. We sincerely prayed that the will of the Lord be done.

Death and Victory

Well, the Lord heard our prayers, for at approximately seven the next morning, as Grandpa calmly rested, his body died and his spirit left him. This was on Monday, May 23, 1983. The Lord had healed him and brought Him home to be with Him, as death was swallowed up in victory.

I must say Grandpa picked a beautiful day to die; a very peaceful and calm day. The sky was blue without a cloud to be seen. The temperature was about 72 degrees. Everyone was at peace, for they knew where he had gone. Sure, there were tears, for we would miss him dearly, but our hearts rejoiced, for we knew where he would spend eternity. Yes, a great warrior had gone home. He had finished his part of the battle. However, he left many strong warriors behind, children he had trained through his lifestyle and his faith in God. His seed was scattered across the world. He has grandchildren and great-grandchildren in Russia, Brazil, Iran and all over the United States.

The wake was held two evenings later, and was unlike any other that I had ever attended. It was

The Final Round

like a big family reunion with people rejoicing, eating, and being merry. Relatives from all over were there, talking and laughing about old times.

Oh, yes, there were tears in some eyes, for his family and friends would miss Grandpa's merry heart and his acts of kindness. But it wasn't long before the tears would be turned to joy, for they knew Grandpa would live for eternity with his heavenly Father. They also knew that his presence and warm kindness would be felt and seen in his children and their children for generations to come.

The day of the funeral was another beautiful day. Many family members met at the funeral home to spend time with one another. From there they followed the hearse to Faith Tabernacle, the church where Grandpa had spent his final twelve years on earth praising God and fellowshipping with the saints.

The first-born grandson of each family was selected to carry the coffin, handsome young men who were now grown. Many had their own families and were successful in many ways.

The coffin was placed in the front of the church and the service began. A group of fifteen people sang some of Grandpa's favorite hymns. Two of them were: "When We've Gone The Last Mile Of The Way," and, "What A Day That Will Be."

The Final Round

This song brought tears to many people's eyes. Grandpa's singing had blessed many people, and this would be one area of his life that would be missed. He sang with all of his might and from his heart, and his influence is of the reasons why the majority of his children and their children sing and play musical instruments.

Grandpa has one son who made a full-play Christian album and all his sons sing special music in various churches. One of his grandsons, S.K. Williams, Jr., has written many Christian songs and is being used of God in the music ministry.

After the singing, the pastor gave a short sermon. He shared how the Godly flourish and prosper. Yes, they see the hard times, but they are steadfast in their service to God. Using Grandpa as an example, he really got his message across. The Pastor pointed out that Grandpa didn't let the pressure of magazines, television, friends, and worldly, ungodly habits dictate to him how he would live his life. With his God—given choice of lifestyle, he chose the godly life, a wise choice. Which do you choose?

When the pastor finished there was a time of prayer for the family, after which the coffin was placed back in the hearse. The funeral procession proceeded to the Faithful Methodist Church Cemetery, about one fourth of a mile from Grandpa's house, where his wives and many other relatives

The Final Round

are buried. It seemed as if the procession was miles long. Relatives and friends from all over took part in it. (The Bible says that he who shows himself friendly will have friends. This was true in Grandpa's life.) Upon arriving at the cemetery, the grandsons carried the coffin to Grandpa's flower-surrounded grave site next to those of his wives. There were hundreds of people gathered around. The final ceremony was performed by his comrades of the V.F.W.

Words of thanks and praise were offered, scriptures were read and final prayers were raised. Buglers played taps and a gun salute rang out into the silent air. As relatives and friends departed, they talked and laughed of good times gone by. Their hearts were not heavy, but at peace, for they were sure of Grandpa's final destiny. I wonder if yours will be known.

Grandpa's body returned to dust from whence it was created, and his spirit returned to God who had given it. His children, grandchildren and great-grandchildren were left to carry on in their earthly toil and walk through life. He left behind one living daughter, five sons, eighteen grandsons, nineteen granddaughters and many great-grandchildren. Each received a godly inheritance as well—a righteous and godly life as their example to live by. Over the years he had divided the fifty acres of land he owned and had given it to his children. Many times he had given to his children and grandchildren money that he had saved.

The Final Round

Many people don't realize the many blessings that the godly man has. We should thank God daily for the blessings we have through Christ.

Grandpa had a very adventuresome childhood. All the way from the hills of Tennessee to the swamps of Louisiana there was adventure in his life. Throughout his marriage he loved God and his wife and children. In his old age he was very active and hard working, was kind, and had a merry heart. I believe and pray that his children and their children from generation to generation will serve, love and honor God, bringing and leaving blessings upon this earth forever and ever. Amen.

For this corruptible must put on incorruption, and this mortal must put on immortality. So when this corruptible shall have put on incorruption, and this mortal shall have put on immortality, then shall be brought to pass the saying that is written, Death is swallowed up in victory. O death, where is thy sting? O grave, where is thy victory? The sting of death is sin, and the strength of sin is the law. But thanks be to God, which giveth us the victory through our Lord Jesus Christ. Therefore, my beloved brethren, be ye steadfast, unmovable, always abounding in the work of the Lord, forasmuch as ye know that your labour is not in vain in the Lord. I Corinthians 15:53-58. (KJV)

And of course it is very good if a man has received wealth from the Lord and good health to enjoy it. To enjoy your work and accept your lot in life is indeed a gift from God. The person who does that will not need to look back with sorrow on his past, for God gives him joy. (See Ecclesiastes 5:19-20 KJV.)

Chapter Seven

Keys to a Successful Life

There are many qualities that bring success to life, and Grandpa had them. I would like to share some with you. First, we must have consistency, endurance and courage in whatever we do.

Another key to a successful life is learning to bring your body under subjection so that you can do the things that you know are right and which you find so hard to do at times. To be a great athlete you must spend many hours in practice and body conditioning. To be great in a specific occupation you must spend hours studying and training. This requires that you be able to control your bodily desires and endure until you accomplish your goals.

The Bible teaches that if we give it shall be given to us. In order to give of yourself you must deny yourself. Great athletes and businessmen give themselves to their sport or job. To be good in a sport you must limit your free time and social events, because you must spend your time training and exercising. The more you give of yourself to meeting your goal, the better you become.

If you want to have a good marriage you must deny yourself and give of your love and time to your family. When you do this you will find that you will receive many blessings in return.

In order to get rich you must give your money away. If you don't invest it, you won't make it. If you want to lose weight you must deny yourself of food and give yourself to less eating.

If you are giving of yourself because of greed or envy or desire for fame, you will not be truly happy with your success. Yes, you will receive your desires, be they riches or fame or beauty. Your inward man, however, will still be perishing and unhappy because the beauty, joy, and fulfillment of life comes from the inward man, not the outward man. The outer man perishes but the inward one lives forever. In order for you to maintain a balanced, happy, successful life you must give of the inward man. You do this because of your love for God and for others, including yourself. When you give from the inner man, your outer man will surely prosper. I think of men who are crippled or paralyzed or poor or old, and yet they are still happy and enjoying life to its fullest. Is this because of the outer man? No, because the outer man is perishing. However, the inner man is still prospering and enjoying life because he has given of himself from the inner man and not of the outer one.

You ask: "How can I give of myself from the inner man?" Romans 3:23 says " For all have sinned, and come short of the glory of God," Romans 6:23 says: "The wages of sin is death; but the gift of God is eternal life through Jesus Christ our Lord." So in order for you to have a happy, successful life with the blessings of God upon it you must receive the gift of God, which is eternal life through Jesus Christ.

I tell you the truth, if you really want to enjoy life, even though the outward, physical being is perishing, you must do it through Jesus Christ. In John 14:6 Jesus said: "...I am the way, the truth, and the life: no man cometh unto the Father but by me." You see, sin separates you from fellowship with your creator. It also keeps you from giving of yourself in love, because without God you cannot have true love. God is love and the author of true love. He loves you so much that He sent His son

Jesus to die for your sins, that you might enjoy fellowshipping with Him and enjoy giving of yourself to Him and others in love.

We are separated from God because of sin, but Jesus is the door through which we can be reunited and restored to God, our Father and Creator. In Revelations 3:20, Jesus said: "Behold, I stand at the door and knock: if any man hear my voice, and open the door, I will come in to him, and will sup with him, and he with me." He truly desires to have fellowship with us, but can't because He is righteous and we are sinful. What fellowship has light with darkness? None. When the light comes in, the darkness leaves. That's why we run from God's word. It is light and it reveals our evil deeds, so we run to the darkness.

It is through Jesus Christ we can come back to the light, because His blood covers our sins. If we repent and confess with our mouths the Lord Jesus and believe in our hearts that He is raised from the dead, we will be saved. (See Romans 10:9.) As a result, the fellowship of the inner man with God will be renewed. In Ephesians 4:23-24 we read: "And be renewed in the spirit of your mind: and that ye put on the new man, which after God is created in righteousness and true holiness."

That's why we must renew our minds daily with the word of God. If we fill our minds with lustful, sinful thoughts, and with movies, magazines, music, etc., we will become lustful, sinful men. However, if we fill our minds with the righteous word of God and with righteous thoughts, we will become righteous men.

Choose this day whom you will serve. The choice is yours. "...but as for me and my house, we will serve the Lord" (Joshua 24:15). If you wish, you can have a happy, successful life through the principles that God has set down for us.

I once asked my Grandpa what he felt was the most important thing in life. He said: "To live an honest Christian life and carry out God's plan for your life." How can you carry out God's plan for your life if you don't know Him and don't have fellowship with Him? We must listen to Him and let Him lead and guide us. Be a hearer and a doer of things that will bring abundant life to you physically, spiritually, and mentally. I pray that you will come to know Him and fellowship with Him so that you can enjoy a happy, successful life and become all that God intended you to be here and in the life to come, just as my Grandpa did.

Also available from the author

One of the most inspiring musical arrangements you will ever hear, "Working and Praying" by Shelby Williams Jr. with special guest Andy Williams on trumpet.

Side One	Side Two
Working and Praying	Momma—A tribute to Moms*
Lay Hold On Eternal Life	Giving It All to Jesus
Attitude of Gratitude	Sing and Shout It
A Fresh Surrender	Worship Jesus
I'm Saved	Bless the Lord While I Live

Working and Praying cost is $8.50 plus $1.50 shipping and handling for cassette and $10.50 plus $1.50 shipping and handling for CD.

* Say it with a song (single): "Momma" is a special tribute to Moms. It comes with a card, envelope and cassette with the words to the song on the inside of the card. **Cost is $4.50 plus $1.50 shipping and handling.**

Additional copies of *My Grandfather's Love* are available for $5.50 plus $1.50 shipping and handling for each book. Send check or money order to:

Purpose Inc.
P.O. Box 1154
44033 Lake Hills Dr.
Prairieville, LA 70769

Phone 504-622-2003 or 504 673-8144

As the need is met, these products are being given to those who need the Truth and the Love of God. Purpose Inc. is a nonprofit organization sharing light and love in a lost and dying world.